Abortion:
What the Founding Fathers Thought About It

by Duane L. Ostler

ISBN-13: 978-1514227992

ISBN-10: 1514227991

Cover - stained glass window designed by Terry Robbins of J. & R. Studios

TABLE OF CONTENTS

This book is dedicated to:

The unborn, who have no choice.

CHAPTER 1: INTRODUCTION

In 1973 the U.S. Supreme Court in *Roe v. Wade* stated that "at the time of the adoption of our Constitution ... abortion was viewed with less disfavor than under most American statutes currently in effect."[1] While the court did not discuss the views of the founding fathers[2] regarding abortion, the implication is clear: abortion was supposedly a commonly accepted practice in 1787 America, and therefore must have likewise been acceptable to the founding fathers themselves.

This book takes issue with any such claim. As will be seen, the founding fathers were firmly against abortion. Furthermore, both colonial statutory law and the common law in that day were also against abortion.

Some today may wonder why the founders' views about abortion and the statutory and common law in their day even matter. After all, the founders are long gone and the world has changed. Those who view the founders' opinion of abortion as unimportant believe that the shift in values from their day to ours justifies abortion. In short, if the founders would have disapproved of abortion, so what? Why would that have any impact on us?

This book also takes issue with such a claim. The founders' views of abortion are extremely relevant to us today, since the constitution they gave us prohibits legalization of abortion and provides for protection of the unborn from the moment of conception. This is due to the Ninth Amendment,[3] which deals with unlisted rights. When the founders adopted the Ninth Amendment, it was their intent and understanding that the unspecified rights it was meant to protect would be derived from natural law as understood in their day[4]--and natural law in that day was very strongly in favor of protecting the unborn from the moment of conception, and was strongly against abortion at any point after conception.[5] Hence, any attempt to derive a constitutional 'right' to an abortion would have been unthinkable to the founders, and directly opposite of natural law. Consequently, they would strongly disagree with the *Roe v. Wade* decision and the legal treatment of abortion in America today.

Notes to chapter 1:

[1] 410 U.S. 113, 140 (1973).

[2] The term 'founding fathers' or 'founders' as used in this book is intended to mean the principal political leaders of the revolutionary and constitutional era, including but not limited to signers of the Declaration of Independence and of the Constitution, as well as the anti-federalists who enlightened the debate about the Constitution with their writings.

[3] The Ninth Amendment states that "The enumeration in the Constitution of certain rights shall not be construed to deny or disparage others retained by the people."

[4] Most scholars who have reviewed the Ninth Amendment agree that the founders

intended it to protect natural rights. *See e.g.,* Bennett B. Patterson, *The Forgotten Ninth Amendment* 19 (1955)("The Ninth Amendment to the Constitution is a basic statement of the inherent natural rights of the individual"); Daniel A. Farber, *Retained by the People: The 'Silent' Ninth Amendment and the Constitutional Rights Americans Don't Know They Have,* 8 (2007)("natural law was not a dead letter for the Founding Fathers; it was hard, enforceable law."); Randy Barnett, "The Ninth Amendment: It Means What it Says," 85 *Texas Law Review* 1, 2 (2006)("The purpose of the Ninth Amendment was to ensure that all individual natural rights had the same stature and force after some of them were enumerated as they had before").

[5] See chapter four, below.

CHAPTER 2: THE FOUNDERS VIEWS ON ABORTION

Statements by the founding fathers demonstrate a universal disapproval of abortion. One of the best demonstrations of disapproval of abortion is from Benjamin Franklin as a young man. By the year 1728, Franklin was working as a partner in a printing business in Philadelphia, which printed handbills and advertisements. He had formerly been employed by another printer in the city, Samuel Keimer, but had parted company under rather unpleasant circumstances. Now, Franklin and Keimer were printing rivals. It came as no surprise then that when Keimer found out Franklin intended to start his own newspaper, Keimer quickly started one of his own to beat him to it. Resentful of what Keimer had done, Franklin then wrote articles for the only other newspaper in the city whereby he "burlesqu'd and ridicul'd" Keimer's paper any way he could.[6] One of the first opportunities that presented itself had to do with abortion.

A portion of Keimer's newspaper was devoted to publishing encyclopedia entries. This was not unusual in that day, in which books and encyclopedias accessible to the public were scarce.[7] Under the letter 'A,' one of the first entries in the encyclopedia that Keimer published was about abortion. Franklin wrote two short rebuttals under the fictitious names of Celia Shortface and Martha Careful who were incensed at Keimer's having discussed abortion openly as if it were a commonly accepted practice approved by the majority. These writings directly contradict the *Roe* court's assertion that abortion was commonly acceptable in that day. In the Shortface piece, Franklin had his character express outrage that "thou would have printed such things in it, as would make all the modest and virtuous women in Pennsylvania ashamed."[8] With typical Franklin humor, the fictitious Martha Careful in her letter threatened that she, "with some others, are resolved to run the hazard of taking him [Keimer] by the beard, at the next place we meet him, and make an example of him for his immodesty."[9] Again, the writings clearly show that abortion was definitely not socially acceptable or approved behavior.

But there is more. It is generally acknowledged that Franklin had an illegitimate son at about the time he was married (1730).[10] As such, Franklin had the opportunity to do what other fathers have done in such circumstances, and so frequently do today--to urge the woman involved to obtain an abortion. Although an example of such an action in that day is extremely rare, and far from the norm in light of the unacceptability of abortion in the founding era, one can be found. In Connecticut in 1742, when Amasa Sessions found that he was responsible for Sarah Grosvenor's pregnancy, he and a claimed doctor, John Hallowell, thereafter tried to convince her to have an abortion. Grosvenor ultimately yielded to their entreaties, but died a month after the crude attempt at abortion by Hallowell in which he used the instruments available to him in that day. Thereafter Hallowell was brought to trial on the charge of attempting to destroy the fetus and endanger Sarah's health. Because proof was uncertain whether Hallowell had been the actual cause of the abortion and the death of the mother, his sentencing upon conviction was for public lashes and two hours on the gallows with a rope around his neck.[11] This case once again confirms the illegality and social unacceptability of abortion in that day.

Franklin could have urged the woman involved in his case to have an abortion, the same as Amasa Sessions and John Hallowell. Or he could have assisted her in committing infanticide, which is discussed more fully in chapter three of this book. But he didn't. Instead, he faced the public shame associated with parenting an illegitimate child in that day, took the boy and raised him himself. To this day the identity of the mother is unknown.[12] Franklin therefore did more than merely issue a written statement against abortion in his newspaper war with Keimer. He showed by his example that he disapproved of abortion and infanticide, even at the price of public shame. A better example of anti-abortion sentiment by a founder could hardly be found.

Franklin's sentiments on preserving infants can also be found in his observations while serving as an ambassador in Paris in 1785. He noted that it was a custom common among Parisians at that time "to pack their infants away, as soon as born, to the Enfans-trouves [foundling homes], with the careless observation that the king is better able to maintain them. I am credibly informed that nine tenths of them die there pretty soon." Franklin decried this "monstrous deficiency of natural affection," and observed that "if parents did not immediately send their infants out of their sight, they would in a few days begin to love them, and thence be spurr'd to greater industry for their maintenance."[13] For Franklin, the Parisian practice was nothing short of common infanticide, and was simply unacceptable.

Franklin was not alone among the founders in discussing the subject of abortion. Thomas Jefferson also wrote about abortions practiced by Native Americans. As part of a description he gave of the practices of some Indians in his day who he characterized as uncivilized savages, he noted that the Indian women would sometimes cause abortion in order to continue accompanying their husbands on war or hunting parties. Based on their very different views regarding life and death, "childbearing becomes extremely inconvenient to them. It is said, therefore, that they have learnt the practice of procuring abortion by the use of some vegetable."[14] While Jefferson was a botanist in his own right and showed tremendous interest in learning about plants and their effects,[15] he demonstrated no interest in knowing just what this 'vegetable' was. Rather, he then commented that civilizing the Indians would dramatically change their abortion practices, since "it is civilization alone which replaces women in the enjoyment of their natural equality."[16] He then noted that "[t]he same Indian women, when married to white traders, who feed them and their children plentifully and regularly, who exempt them from excessive drudgery, who keep them stationary and unexposed to accident, produce and raise as many children as the white women."[17] The main point for Jefferson was that only an unprincipled savage would engage in an abortion.

Another example of a founder's views regarding abortion is a narrative written by John Adams extolling the virtues of Lycurgus, the legendary Greek political reformer, said to have lived in the 7th century BC. Adams noted that Lycurgus was on the verge of succeeding to the throne at the death of his brother

Polydectes, "but being told his brother's widow was with child, he declared himself protector only, and resigned the crown."[18] However, his brother's widow offered to have an abortion to "remove out of his way the only competitor" to the throne.[19] Adams recounts how Lycurgus then "deceived her by counterfeited tenderness; and diverted her from the thoughts of an abortion, by promising to take the disposition of the child upon himself when it should be born."[20] Adams was clearly impressed with Lycurgus, and his refusal to allow the proposed abortion. On another occasion, Adams lamented the cruelty of British soldiers, citing as an example how in an invasion of Brittanny in 1761 "six soldiers ripped open with a knife a woman big with child ... the English gave a free course to their cruelty, and indulged themselves in all sorts of excesses, which the laws of war reprobate as well as those of nature."[21] For Adams, abortion in any form was simply unacceptable, and contrary to the laws of nature.

Benjamin Rush is another founder whose comments show that he would not agree with abortion at any point after conception. Rush was one of the signers of the Declaration of Independence, and was also a doctor. He stated that life's "first motion is produced by the stimulus of the male seed upon the female ovum ... No sooner is the female ovum thus set in motion, and the foetus formed, than its capacity of life is supported."[22] Rush commented further on the constant movement by the unborn from the moment of conception, supported in the first trimester by the heat it received from its mother and its own blood circulation, and then later "[b]y its constant motion in the womb after the third month of pregnancy. The absence of this motion for a few days is always a sign of the indisposition or death of a foetus."[23] For Rush, the life of the unborn began at conception and merited protection thereafter.

Rush's understanding was consistent with others in the medical profession of that era. An example is seen in a book for midwives and doctors on how to treat and prevent spontaneous abortion by Dr. John Burns in England, in 1806. Regarding purposely induced abortion and the life of the infant, Dr. Burns said the following:

Such medicines, likewise, as exert a violent action on the stomach or bowels will, upon the principle formerly mentioned, frequently excite abortion; and very often are taken designedly for that purpose in such quantity as to produce fatal effects; and here I must remark, that many people at least pretend to view attempts to excite abortion as different from murder, upon the principle that the embryo is not possessed of life, in the common acceptation of the word. It undoubtedly can neither think nor act; but, upon the same reasoning, we should conclude it to be innocent to kill the child in the birth. Whoever prevents life from continuing, until it arrive at perfection, is certainly as culpable as if he had taken it away after that it had been accomplished.[24]

In 1716, the Common Council of New York City enacted an ordinance directed at midwives which stated that "you shall not give any counsel or administer any herb medicine or potion or any other thing to any woman being with child whereby she should destroy or miscarry."[25] This law had been on the books for fully 60 years prior to the American Revolution. Scholars have noted that this law was similar to others enacted in England regarding midwives as early as 1512.[26]

Other founders made references to the subject of abortion which were also very enlightening. Hugh Hughes, one of the sons of liberty and quartermaster from New York during the Revolution, wrote an article published in The New York Journal in 1788 during the debate on whether to adopt the

Constitution. Among other things, he expounded on the evils of a poll tax--a fee that voters would have to pay in order to vote. In his first draft of the article before it was published, he stated at one point that "the term 'person' may include every human creature, whether born or unborn." He then asserted that a poll tax would therefore apply to the unborn, which might "produce a right of celibacy or not marrying in the one sex, and that of procuring abortions in the other."[27] The wording of Hughes' article was changed slightly by the time it was published. In the final publication, the poll tax reference remained unchanged but the wording after it was changed to read, "may produce a right of celibacy or not marrying in the one sex, and something worse in the other, at least something more criminal in the eyes of the law."[28] This was an incredibly clear statement regarding the criminal nature of abortion as seen by the founders.

On other occasions, the founders used the term 'abortion' in a negative sense to describe self destructive actions. For example, James Madison used the term in referring to the unwise combining of the question of where to locate the national capital with other issues, which could end in "an abortion of both."[29] Alexander Hamilton used the term to describe the unsuccessful British attempt to tax tea imported to the American colonies, which resulted in the Boston Tea Party.[30] And George Washington used the term to describe what would happen if each of the states were to attempt to regulate commerce on their own.[31]

As for contraception, once again the founders spoke very little about it. However, that does not mean they knew nothing of the subject or objected to pre-conception methods *between husband and wife*. It is important to note however that they would never approve of sex out of wedlock, or the use of contraception as a method to aid the promiscuity we see so commonly today. James Wilson described the founders' views on this subject when he described the practice of sex out of wedlock in ancient Rome as "that detestable train of conjugal vice, infidelity, rage, rancor and revenge with which so many volumes of the Roman story are crowded and disgraced."[32]

Again however, contraception methods within marriage undertaken prior to conception were not objected to by the founders. Condoms made of animal parts had been known for centuries in Europe.[33] Other methods of contraception also existed. For example, Theodore Sedgewick, a member of the House of Representatives in the first Congress, noted that his wife had breast-fed one of their children far longer than was necessary, apparently as a birth control method.[34] Indeed, James Madison likewise referred to extended breast feeding as a method of birth control.[35] One scholar has noted that "Women's diaries and letters written in the eighteenth or nineteenth centuries record their reliance on extended periods of breast feeding to space pregnancies."[36] Abigail Adams commented on the large number of children some of her relatives were having, thereby implying that they should have done something to prevent it.[37] Yet Abigail, like her husband John, would never have agreed to abortion as a method of birth control. She was greatly traumatized by the stillbirth of one of her children, and explained that it "was not owing to any injury which I had sustained, nor could any care of mine have prevented it."[38]

One scholar researching fertility in the founding era found that birth rates dropped significantly after 1750 as compared to the rest of the world, and continued to drop throughout the entirety of the founding era.[39] Specifically she found that more than half of the 56 signers of the Declaration of Independence had 6 or fewer children. This was still a large family by today's standards, but was a great reduction from the average family size prior to that time, of about 10 to 12 children.[40] Obviously, this reduction was due to contraception practices between husband and wife during this era, but not abortion which was clearly unacceptable to the founding generation.

There is tremendous consistency in the founders' support of contraception within marriage, but objection to abortion. Family size and whether to create life in the first instance are matters of choice. There is nothing unnatural in a couple taking reasonable steps to prevent conception. But in the view of the founders, once life has its start and conception has occurred, it merits ongoing protection from that point on.

Notes to chapter 2:

[6] Benjamin Franklin, *The Autobiography of Benjamin Franklin*, 62 (1771).

[7] It was precisely this situation that led Franklin to join with others in forming the first public library in the colonies. Ibid at 78.

[8] *A Benjamin Franklin Reader* 46 (Walter Isaacson, ed., 2003).

[9] Ibid at 45.

[10] John T. Morse, *Benjamin Franklin*, 15-16 (1889); Esmond Wright, *Franklin of Phildadelphia*, 41-43 (1986). Wright indicates that Franklin's common-law marriage to Deborah Read (rather than regular marriage) was because her first husband was still alive, although his location was unknown.

[11] The story of Grosvenor, Sessions and Hallowell is recounted in: Joseph W. Dellapenna, *Dispelling the Myths of Abortion History* 221-224 (2006). Hallowell fled the colony before the sentence was carried out.

[12] Morse, above note 10, at 16; Wright, above note 10, at 42-43.

[13] Letter of May 23, 1785 to George Wheatley, found in Benjamin Franklin and William Duane, *Memoirs of Benjamin Franklin,* vol. 1, at 589-590 (1840).

[14] *The Writings of Thomas Jefferson,* vol. 3, at 153 (Paul Leicester Ford, ed., 1892-99).

[15] For example, Jefferson communicated frequently in 1813 with his friend Samuel Brown regarding a variety of different plants. On one occasion Jefferson showed special interest in the deadly herb Datura Stromonium, which could cause death as quietly as sleep. He expressed the opinion that "there are ills in life as desperate as intolerable, to which it would be the rational relief, e.g., the inveterate cancer." Letter to Dr. Samuel Brown,

July 14, 1813, found in *The Papers of Thomas Jefferson,* vol. 6, at 293 (J. Jefferson Looney ed., 2009).

[16] Ford, above note 14, at 153.

[17] Ibid at 154.

[18] *The Works of John Adams,* vol. 4, at 549 (Charles Francis Adams ed., 1851).

[19] Ibid.

[20] Ibid.

[21] Letter of John Adams to the President of the Continental Congress, Dec. 30, 1780, found in: *The Revolutionary Diplomatic Correspondence of the United States,* vol. 4, at 215 (Francis Wharton, ed., 1889).

[22] *The Selected Writings of Benjamin Rush,* at 151 (Dagovert D. Runes, ed., 1947)(emphasis added).

[23] Ibid.

[24] John Burns, *Observations on Abortion* at 65-66 (1806).

[25] 'A Law for Regulating Mid Wives within the City of New York, July 27, 1716,' found in Minutes of the Common Council of the City of New York, at 352-55 (1675-1776). For a discussion of other such laws and abortion court cases in the colonial era, see: Marvin Olasky, Abortion Rites: A Social History of Abortion in America (1992).

[26] Dennis J. Horan & Thomas J. Marzen, "Abortion and Midwifery: A Footnote in Legal History," found in Thomas W. Hilgers, Dennis J. Horan and David Mall, *New Perspectives on Human Abortion*, at 199-200 (1981).

[27] *The Documentary History of the Ratification of the Constitution Digital Edition*, at 664 (John P. Kaminski, Gaspare J. Saladino,

Richard Leffler, Charles H. Schoenleber & Margaret A. Hogan, eds., U. of Va. Press, 2009)(Last accessed July 31, 2013).

[28] Ibid.

[29] *The Writings of James Madison*, vol. 6, at 14 (Gaillard Hunt ed., 1900).

[30] *The Works of Alexander Hamilton*, vol. 2, at 93 (John C. Hamilton, ed., 1850). Hamilton discussed how the British ministry reacted when their tea tax idea backfired, stating "[t]he abortion of their favorite plan, inflamed the ministerial ire."

[31] Letter of Nov. 30, 1785 to David Stuart, *The Writings of George Washington*, vol. 28, at 328 (John C. Fitzpatrick ed., 1938). Washington stated that "[t]he resolutions which were published for consideration, vesting Congress with powers to regulate the

Commerce of the Union, have I hope been acceded to. If the States individually were to attempt this, an abortion, or a many headed Monster would be the issue."

[32] *The Works of James Wilson*, vol. 2, at 600 (Robert G. McCloskey ed., 1967).

[33] Janet Farrell Brodie, *Contraception and Abortion in Nineteenth Century America*, at 27 (1994).

[34] Ibid. at 46.

[35] Hunt, above note 29, vol. 9, at 54. Madison was speaking of a book by William Godwin, just published, in which Godwin asserted that the United States population was not rising significantly. The statement was made in reference to Indian tribes in Paraguay, and some of the reasons they were not increasing in population.

[36] Dellapenna, above note 11, at 73.

[37] Ibid. at 41.

[38] Edith B. Gelles, *Abigail and John: Portrait of a Marriage*, 105 (2009). John Adams was also very upset. "I feel a Grief and Mortification, that is heightened tho it is not wholly occasioned, by my sympathy with the mother." Ibid. at 106.

[39] Susan E. Klepp, *Revolutionary Conceptions: Women, Fertility and Family Limitation in America* 1760-1820, 26 (2009).

[40] Ibid. at 18.

CHAPTER 3: CONCEALMENT LAWS: ABORTION AS A SUBSET OF INFANTICIDE

The majority in *Roe v. Wade* made a serious historical error in the following statement, in which they asserted that abortion laws are of relatively recent origin:

> [T]he restrictive criminal abortion laws in effect in a majority of States today are of relatively recent vintage. Those laws, generally proscribing abortion or its attempt at any time during pregnancy except when necessary to preserve the pregnant woman's life, are not of ancient or even of common-law origin. Instead,

they derive from statutory changes effected, for the most part, in the latter half of the 19th century.[41]

This is not accurate, at least in respect to illegitimate children. In 1623, fully 150 years before the American Revolution and 350 years before the *Roe* court made its bizarre statement, the British Parliament enacted "An Act to Prevent the Destroying and Murdering of Bastard Children."[42] The separate reference to "destroying" and "murdering" draws the distinction between abortion and infanticide, both of which were covered by the law. A 'bastard' child is, of course, an illegitimate child, born out of wedlock. This act "presumed murder from concealment of the death of a bastard in order to conceal its birth."[43] Again, the law dealt with both infanticide and abortion, which were lumped together as equally horrific crimes. One scholar has noted that ten American colonies or early states enacted similar laws, and that in fact "the English concealment statute was received in the colonies as part of the common law."[44] The 'common law' is the British traditional law used by courts in their decisions when they have no other law to turn to. In Pennsylvania between the years of 1682 and 1800 there were 57 women prosecuted under that colony's concealment law.[45] These concealment laws, generally accepted throughout the American colonies, were very strict against abortion. It should be noted that concealment laws in England were not repealed until 1803--by the same statute that first made abortion illegal in that country.

A revision to New York's concealment law in 1787 was commented on by Alexander Hamilton. His statement shows that he supported charging unwed women with murder who aborted their children. The debate was about a revision to New York's concealment law pertaining to unwed mothers, under which "women who clandestinely were delivered of children and the same die, *or be born dead*, that the mother within one month thereafter, should before a magistrate be obliged to produce one witness at least, to prove that the child was not murdered; and in default of concealing the same, to be deemed guilty of murder."[46] The plain reference to "or be born dead" indicated that this law applied directly to abortion.

The main problem with the law of course was that it reversed the presumption that a person is innocent until proven guilty, forcing single women who gave birth to prove their innocence. If they failed to do so, their guilt was considered as established, and the punishment followed. It is not surprising therefore that Hamilton opposed this law since he believed it could condemn the innocent as well as the guilty. He "expatiated feelingly on the delicate situation it placed an unfortunate woman in, *who might by accident be delivered stillborn.*"[47] He offered no argument on behalf of women whose stillbirth was *not* accidental (ie, abortion). But regarding the accidental stillbirth of a woman who was clearly guilty of fornication or adultery but not murder, "the operation of this law compelled her to publish her shame to the world" in order to avoid a murder conviction. Because the clandestine birth would in most cases be unknown to all but a few, he noted that "she would prefer the danger of punishment from concealment, to the avowal of her guilt."[48] The simple reality is that this anti-abortion law suffered from a serious due process problem because of its presumption of guilt. For this reason, Hamilton considered the proposed revision to be "neither politic or just."[49]

Thomas Jefferson also opposed the concealment law in Virginia in 1778, raising similar concerns to those voiced by Hamilton. His comments show that--like Hamilton--he was troubled by the concealment law's effect of lumping together both the guilty and the innocent, since the law presumed guilt solely based on concealment by the mother of a dead child. He noted that "[s]o many children die before or soon after birth that to presume all those murdered who are found dead, is a presumption which will lead us oftener wrong than right, and consequently would shed more blood than it would save ... If the child were born dead, the mother would naturally choose rather to conceal it, in hopes of still keeping a good character in the neighborhood."[50] Like Hamilton, Jefferson was not troubled with a charge of murder against a woman who, either by abortion before its birth or infanticide after the birth, took the life of the child; rather, it was the law's presumption of guilt based on concealment alone that was unacceptable, since it also condemned single women with legitimate stillborn children, and was therefore a blatant violation of due process. Jefferson acknowledged that "[t]he crime is difficult to prove, being usually committed in secret."[51] For him the law simply went too far. He preferred that such matters of proof should not be presumed, but should be referred to a "jury, who are, in a regular course, to hear presumptive, as well as positive testimony."[52] A jury could rely on better evidence: "circumstantial proof will do; for example, marks of violence, the behavior, countenance, &c., of the prisoner, &c."[53] These comments by Jefferson confirm his negative view of the abortions practiced by Native Americans, as discussed above. Viewing abortion as essentially the same crime as infanticide also sheds great light on the view expressed by Jefferson's close associate, James Madison, who condemned infant life being "destroyed by infanticide, as among the Chinese."[54]

The link between infanticide and abortion is further solidified in notes prepared by John Marshall in 1793, when he was an attorney representing Nancy Randolph. John Marshall was one of the founders from Virginia who later became a famous Supreme Court justice. At issue in the 1793 case was an accusation of infanticide against Nancy and Richard Randolph, who were distant relatives of each other, and part of the prominent Randolph family in Virginia. Unmarried Nancy Randolph, whose brother was married to Thomas Jefferson's daughter Martha, was suspected of infanticide of an illegitimate son, allegedly said to have been fathered by Richard Randolph, another member of the family.[55] In order to quiet the scandal and prove the innocence of himself and Nancy, Richard arranged to submit to questioning before the Cumberland County Court on the matter. Both Richard and Nancy were questioned, and both were ultimately acquitted upon the conclusion that the child was naturally stillborn and not due to abortion.[56]

The evidence before the Cumberland Court clearly indicates that this was an abortion case, even though the official charge was for infanticide. Among the evidence produced in the case was a statement by Martha (Jefferson's daughter) that she had spoken with Nancy at one point about some of her ongoing health problems. They discussed a drug called 'Gum Guicaum,' which was said to be "an excellent medicine for the cholic, but observed at the same time that it was dangerous medicine, as it would produce an abortion."[57] Upon Nancy's request, Martha sent Nancy some Gum Guiacum, but because Martha suspected Nancy was pregnant the amount she sent was "not in a considerable quantity. She [Martha] has known more to be given to a pregnant woman, without producing any mischief."[58] Hence, Martha refused to provide sufficient Gum Guiacum to produce an abortion, even though she knew her sister-in-law faced public scandal if the suspected pregnancy became known. Furthermore, in notes prepared by John Marshall (who was a relative of the Randolphs) in preparation for his possible defense of Nancy, Marshall argued that Nancy took the drug for her other health problems and did not desire or attempt an abortion with the drug--again in spite of the scandal she might otherwise face. He argued that if "she sought to procure abortion it would have been in the early state of her pregnancy," not on the verge of birth while she was visiting a relative's house.[59] In so saying, Marshall was not suggesting that a prior attempt at abortion would have been acceptable, but was merely offering a logical lawyer's argument against the accusation at issue--which was that Nancy had caused the child to be stillborn (i.e., had aborted the child) through use of Gum Guiacum shortly before its birth. Again, the most telling point of this argument is that Richard and Nancy were accused of infanticide,[60] but Martha Jefferson's comments and Marshall's arguments on Nancy's behalf all had to do with abortion. They and others involved in the case viewed the two as essentially the same crime.

In sum, statements by the founders regarding 'concealment' laws which were targeted at infanticide and abortion by unwed mothers confirm their disapproval of abortion. The understanding of the founders was that abortion was a mere subset of infanticide, and was equally unacceptable with it.

Notes to chapter 3:

[41] *Roe v. Wade*, 410 US 113, 129 (1973).

[42] 21. Jac. I. c. 27, found in *Statutes at Large, 39 Eliz. to 12 Charles*, vol. 7, at 298 (Danby Pickering ed., 1763). The presumption of murder under concealment laws was finally repealed in England in 1803--by the same statute that first made abortion illegal in that

country. Dellapenna, above note 11, at 100-107.

[43] 21. Jac. I. c. 27, above note 42.

[44] Dellapenna, above note 11, at 116-17.

[45] Ibid, at 121.

[46] *The Papers of Alexander Hamilton*, vol. 4, at 39 (Harold C. Syrett & Jacob E. Cooke eds., 1962)(emphasis added).

[47] Ibid (emphasis added).

[48] Ibid.

[49] Ibid.

[50] *The Jeffersonian Cyclopedia*, at 598 (John P. Foley ed., 1900).

[51] Ibid.

[52] Ibid.

[53] Ibid. The marks of violence could be on the dead child or on the woman as an attempted abortion, since beating a woman's

stomach was one method of attempted abortion in that day.

[54] Hunt, above note 29, vol. 6, at 48.

[55] The background of this case is summarized in an editorial note in: *The Papers of John Marshall,* vol. 2, at 161-68 (Charles T. Cullen & Herbert A. Johnson eds., 1977).

[56] Ibid.

[57] Ibid. at 168-69.

[58] Ibid. at 169.

[59] Ibid. at 177.

[60] In a history of Patrick Henry, hired to represent Richard Randolph, it is stated that the charge against Richard "was the murder of a newly-born infant, of which he was the reputed father." William Wirt Henry, *Patrick Henry, Life, Correspondence and Speeches,* vol. 2, at 491 (1891).

Duane L. Ostler

CHAPTER 4: JOHN LOCKE AND OTHER NATURAL LAW WRITERS ON ABORTION

In addition to their own statements given above, the views of the founders on abortion can also be found by reviewing what the natural law writers they revered had to say about it. As noted above, this is extremely significant, since the founders believed the Ninth Amendment incorporated natural law into the Constitution. Interestingly, most of the natural law writers who were read and quoted by the founders wrote on these topics, including John Locke. These natural law writers identified abortion as a violation of natural law from the moment of conception.

It cannot be overemphasized that the founders were very familiar with these writings, and indeed relied heavily on natural law in justifying their break from England--based on the natural law right of the people to revolt against a tyrannical government. The concept was stated clearly by Jefferson in the Declaration of Independence, in which he referred to "the laws of nature and of Nature's God" in justifying "the right of the people to alter or abolish" the tyrannical government over them.[61] The founders enshrined natural law in the Ninth Amendment, which most scholars agree was based on natural law rights.[62] If any unlisted right was to be derived from the constitution--as the *Roe* court did in ignoring the rights of the unborn and 'finding' a 'right' to have an abortion--the founders intended that such a right would be derived from their understanding of natural rights, through the Ninth Amendment.[63] Hence, the rights identified by natural law writers are of great importance in the abortion debate. The founding fathers were intimately familiar with the writings of the natural law theorists of their day, and firmly believed in the natural law rights these writers identified.

The founders frequently identified which natural law writers they primarily studied and which they believed expressed the most compelling ideas. Alexander Hamilton for example, in criticizing the writings of British-supporter Samuel Seabury in 1775, advised him to "[a]pply yourself, without delay, to the study of the law of nature. I would recommend to your perusal, Grotius, Pufendorf, Locke, Montesquieu, and Burlemaqui."[64] James Otis in his speeches before the revolution often cited Pufendorf, Grotius, Barbeyrac and Burlamaqui.[65] James Wilson in his lecture on "Of the Natural Rights of Individuals" referred to these same classical writers.[66]

The best known of all the natural law writers relied on by the founders was John Locke. It is very curious that Locke's statements against abortion--which were undoubtedly well known to the founders--have been so universally ignored in modern times. Locke classified abortion as being one of several actions that are wrong under the laws of nature whether they are acknowledged as wrong by men or not. His list of such actions was "not to kill another man; not to know more women than one; not to procure abortion; not to expose their children; not to take from another what is his ..."[67]

But Locke said more. He acknowledged that the life of the unborn commences at conception and is therefore a person even if it dies in the womb. He said that "the body of an embryo, dying in the womb, may be very little, not the thousandth part of an ordinary man. For since from the first conception and beginning of formation, it has life."[68] This is an incredibly strong and profound statement from the natural law writer who had such a tremendous influence on the founding fathers.[69]

Locke also wrote strongly against the notion that a parent--most especially a father in that day--had power over the life and death of his children:

The argument, I have heard others make use of, to prove that fathers, by begetting them, come by an absolute power over their children, is this; that fathers have a power over the lives of their children, because they give them life and being ... To give life to that which has yet no being, is to frame and make a living creature, fashion the parts, and mould and suit them to their uses, and having proportioned and fitted them together, to put into them a living soul. He that could do this, might indeed have some pretence to destroy his own workmanship. But is there any one so bold, that dares thus far arrogate to himself the incomprehensible works of the almighty?[70]

Hence, Locke viewed life from the time of conception as a sacred gift from God, not to be trifled with by men. Even the parents of the child had no right to deny its right to life.

Other natural law writers also spoke against abortion. Samuel von Pufendorf was the most prolific in writing on this subject. For example, in speaking of those who have no rights because they are not yet "a part of the world," he stated: "[n]ow by him who is not yet a part of the world we understand one who has not yet been conceived, not one who is still in the womb."[71] This is an incredibly clear statement from one of the most influential of the natural law writers of the founding era that the unborn had rights from the moment of conception. On another occasion, he stated, "Obligation has also been enjoined upon parents by the law of nature, that not merely shall they not destroy by abortion the offspring conceived within their flesh, nor expose it, nor put it to death after it has been brought into the light of day; but also that they shall supply it with nourishment (one or both of them, just as they have agreed in the marriage pact), until it can conveniently support itself."[72] Like Locke, Pufendorf named abortion and infanticide one after the other, each equally unacceptable.

But there was more. Pufendorf also offered the following insight, where abortion was procured in order to avoid public shame:

For the life of the babe was guarded not only by the mother instinct but by law;

and the mother should have recognized before the event that her infamy was of less consequence than the death of one whose existence was due to an act to which she herself had consented. Wherefore, if the care for her reputation meant more to her than the pleasure of copulation or the love of her own offspring, she ought to have been thinking about the matter before she took the man to herself. *After the act*, the child does not merit death, in order that the sin of the parent may go unobserved.[73]

Once more, this was an amazingly clear statement that any attempt to destroy the fetus after intercourse was completely unacceptable. Indeed, it almost sounds as if it was written by a modern day anti-abortionist, and expresses what many in modern times have asserted--that abstinence among the unmarried is the responsible behavior, not abortion.

Pufendorf also made comments that were applicable to contraception practiced by married couples. He noted that "he who becomes parent of few children satisfies the law of nature as well as he who becomes the parent of many."[74] He also stated that "to force a man to beget children to no hope but that of hunger is inhuman, and to fill a state with a crowd of beggars is improvident."[75] Yet, as we have already seen above, he firmly believed that abortion was not the method to avoid this result. Obviously, contraception by married couples or abstinence by the unmarried was the proper way.

Locke and Pufendorf were not alone among natural law writers in speaking against abortion. The French natural law writer Montesquieu condemned abortion in his 1721 social commentary novel 'The Persian Letters.' In a chapter devoted to uncivilized savages (a reference reminiscent of Jefferson's observations about savages, above), Montesquieu stated the following regarding the barbarity of abortion:

There is among savages another custom ... it is the cruel practice of abortion to which their women are addicted, in order that pregnancy may not render them distasteful to their husbands.[76]

Montesquieu went on to say that in Paris "the laws enacted against this crime are terribly harsh."[77] He then described the Parisian law, which was essentially the same concealment law as that in England discussed above, which pertained to unmarried women concealing the death of newborn children.[78] (An effort to dodge this Parisian law may be the reason newborns were often sent to 'foundling homes' where they died in droves as noted by Benjamin Franklin, rather than being aborted). In short then, Montesquieu likewise viewed abortion as repugnant and criminal.

Other natural law writers relied on by the founding fathers also condemned abortion. For example, Jean-Jacques Burlemaqui stated as follows:

... the right which requires that nobody should injure or offend us, belongs as well to children, and even to infants that are still in their mother's wombs, as to adult persons. This is the foundation of that equitable rule of the Roman law, which declares, That infants who are as yet in their mothers wombs, are considered as already brought into the world, whenever the question relates to anything that may turn to their advantage.[79]

Hugo Grotius made a similar statement. He noted that "children yet unborn are considered as already born, whenever their advantage is in question."[80] Neither Burlemaqui or Grotius made any attempt to qualify this protection, to depend on the trimester of the fetus--in other words, how long the infant was in the womb. The concept Burlemaqui and Grotius were expressing is quite straightforward: if there is ever any doubt or question about abortion, do that which errs on the side of protection. Indeed, what could be more natural and to the 'advantage' or 'favor' of an unborn—at any stage of pregnancy—than to have its life preserved?

In sum, natural law writers Locke, Pufendorf, Montesquieu, Burlamaqui and Grotius were in agreement that abortion at ANY stage of pregnancy was contrary to the law of nature, and that the unborn should be protected from the moment of conception. These were the types of things read by the founders, and with which they most heartily agreed. And these are the natural law principles on which the rights of the unborn as well as any alleged 'right' pertaining to abortion can be derived from the Ninth Amendment.

Accordingly, if the *Roe* court had properly applied the Ninth Amendment regarding the unlisted 'right' to have an abortion in the way intended by the founders, they would have ruled opposite to the way they did. However, they ignored the Ninth Amendment and the natural law rights of the unborn, and instead 'derived' the right to an abortion from the Fourteenth Amendment's due process clause. There is no basis for this, since the drafters of the Fourteenth Amendment never contemplated that it would be used to support unlisted rights in the constitution. That is the job of the Ninth Amendment alone.

Notes to chapter 4:

[61] Declaration of Independence, ¶ 1, 2.

[62] Above note 4, and authorities cited therein.

[63] For a deeper discussion of the founders' understanding of the Ninth Amendment see: Duane L. Ostler, "Rights under the Ninth Amendment: Not that Hard to Identify After All," 7(1) *Federal Courts Law Review* 35 (2013).

[64] Syrett & Cooke, above note 46, vol. 1, at 86.

[65] John Adams and Jonathan Sewell, *Novanglus and Massachusettensis; or Political Essays, Ppublished in the Years 1774 and 1775*, 230 (1968)(1819). Barbeyrac was primarily a translator of the works of Grotius and Pufendorf.

[66] McCloskey, above note 32, vol. 2, at 585 et seq.

[67] John Locke, *The Works of John Locke in Nine Volumes*, vol. 1, at 48 (12th ed., 1824)(ch3, sec.19).

[68] See 'Mr. Locke's Reply to the Right Reverend the Lord Bishop of Worcester's Answer to his Second Letter, Ibid., at 311. Locke was arguing against the Bishop of Worcester's claim that in the resurrection there is no growth, noting that if this is so, an embryo dying in the womb "must, according to your Lordship's doctrine, remain a man not an inch long to eternity." Ibid.

[69] Scholars have frequently noted Locke's influence on the founders. For a sampling, see: John C. Miller, *Origins of the American Revolution* 170-76 (2d ed., 1966); Donald L. Doernberg, "'We the People': John Locke, Collective Constitutional Rights, and Standing

to Challenge Government Action," 73 *California Law Review* 52 (1985); David L. Wardle, "Reason to Ratify: The Influence of John Locke's Religious Beliefs on the Creation and Adoption of the United States Constitution," 26 *Seattle University Law Review* 291 (2002).

[70] Locke, above note 67, vol. 4, at 251 (Ch. 6, sec.'s 52 & 53).

[71] Samuel Pufendorf, *De Jure Naturae Et Genium Libri Octo* (Eight Books on Natural Rights), vol. 2, at 657 (C.H. Oldfather & W.A. Oldfather, transl., 1934)(1688)(found in Bk 4, Ch 12, sec. 10).

[72] Samuel Pufendorf, *Elementorum Jurisprudentiae Universalis* [The Elements of Universal Jurisprudence], vol. 2, at 283 (William A. Oldfather trans., 1931)(1660).

[73] Pufendorf, *De Jure Naturae*, above note 71, vol. 2, at 841 (Bk 6, Ch 1, sec. 3, 'on matrimony')(emphasis added).

[74] Ibid., at 841.

[75] Ibid., at 851.

[76] Charles de Secondat, baron de Montesquieu, *The Persian Letters*, 218 (1721)(1901, Herat ed).

[77] Ibid.

[78] Ibid. In the footnote, Montesquieu described the law thus: "Every unmarried woman who has not declared her pregnancy before a magistrate is punished with death if her offspring dies. Shame and the sense of her dishonor, even accidents, are not accepted in extenuation." Ibid. An effort to dodge this law may be the reason Parisian children were sent to 'foundling homes' as noted by Benjamin

Franklin, although sending to such homes was apparently also the method of infanticide practiced by the married women of Paris. See *Not Your Usual Founding Father: Selected Readings from Benjamin Franklin*, 21-22 (Edmund S. Morgan ed., 2006).

[79] Jean-Jacques Burlemaqui, *The Principles of Natural and Political Law*, at 84-85 (Petter Korkman, ed., 2006)(1747)(emphasis in original)(Found at Part 1, Ch7, section 7)(Translated by Thomas Nugent).

[80] Hugo Grotius, *Introduction to Dutch Jurisprudence*, Ch. III, sec. 4, XVL.

CHAPTER 5: THE EVIDENTIARY NATURE OF THE COMMON LAW ABORTION RULE

As can be seen from the above, the founders' sentiments regarding abortion are abundantly evident both in their own writings and in the writings of the natural law writers they believed in. Yet interestingly, when the views of the founders regarding abortion are discussed, usually the only founder cited is James Wilson and his quoting of the common law abortion rule expressed by the preeminent British legal scholar, William Blackstone.

Once again, the 'common law' is the law courts use when there is no other law on a particular subject. It is derived from British traditions and court decisions going back hundreds of years. While the British common law did indeed address the subject of abortion, the *Roe* court's interpretation of the common law abortion rule is grossly in error, as we shall see.

Citing Blackstone, James Wilson stated that "human life, from its commencement to its close, is protected by the common law. *In the contemplation of law*, life begins when the infant is first able to stir in the womb. (1 Blackstone's Commentaries, 129) By the law, life is protected not only from immediate destruction, but from every degree of actual violence, and, in some cases, from every degree of danger."[81] Reading this, it almost seems that under the British common law, abortion was criminal only after outwardly observable 'quickening' or stirring of the infant in the womb (roughly almost half way through pregnancy), and not before, because that is when life 'began.' Indeed, that is how the *Roe* court interpreted it. As we shall see however, the common law rule was *not* based on philosophical notions of when life began as claimed by the *Roe* majority.[82] Instead, the rule was solely one of evidence. The point of the rule was that a criminal conviction for abortion became possible only when movement of the fetus could be verified to a court of law, which in that day was at 'quickening.' Prior to quickening, proof sufficient to put someone in jail for life or execute them for abortion was simply lacking. Obviously then, *the common law rule was actually designed to protect the unborn from the moment that fetal movement could be verified.*

Accordingly, we can see that the comment from Wilson was an articulation of the strictly legal, evidentiary rule to be followed in the few abortion cases not already covered by the concealment statutes. Recall that the concealment laws pertained to abortions by unmarried pregnant women. Hence, the common law abortion rule of 'quickening' was to apply only to abortions by married women. And once again, *in the contemplation of law*, proof sufficient for a criminal conviction due to abortion required evidence that the child was 'quickened' and therefore alive and moving. In those days of limited medical technology, quickening or movement of the child (usually occurring around the 16th to 20th week of pregnancy) was practically the only way to confirm the child was alive. This has already been described in the statement from Dr. Benjamin Rush above, that movement of the fetus could not be outwardly detected until well into the second trimester.[83] Under the common law, anything done to purposefully stop the movement of the child from the time such movement was detected would be criminal. But even then a conviction may not rise to the level of murder since it was always possible, in those days when spontaneous abortion was common and medical technology could not prove the cause of death, that the abortionist's efforts were not the actual cause of the abortion. This was seen in the Hallowell case, discussed above, in which the doctor had clearly attempted an abortion, but it was unknown whether he had actually caused one. For this reason, his penalty upon conviction, although severe, was less than it would have been for murder.[84]

On the other hand, abortive acts prior to quickening would not necessarily "in the contemplation of law" result in a criminal conviction, since it would be impossible to prove whether the child was alive (and often whether the woman was even pregnant) when the act occurred. Hence, due process and fairness compelled the common law rule, which was all based on provable fetal movement. It again should not be forgotten that stillborns were common in those days, and therefore proof (especially for something as serious as a murder charge) was a significant issue in any criminal proceeding regarding abortion.

Scholars have noted that "[t]he primitive nature of biological knowledge and abortion technology made it next to impossible to prove that the child was alive before the supposed abortion and that the abortion was the cause of death."[85] Furthermore, "[e]arly writers on the law focused their discussion of abortion on the evidentiary impossibility of determining whether a woman was pregnant and of determining whether the fetus was still alive when an abortionist began."[86] James Parker, who summarized the common law in New York in 1764, cited Lord Hale for the proposition that in an abortion case "it cannot be *legally known*, whether the child were killed or not."[87]

An early example of the evidentiary purpose behind the common law rule is found in the

1348 *'Abortionist's Case'* in England, in which an indictment against a person for killing an unborn child was refused because "it is difficult to know whether he killed the child or not."[88] A similar result was reached in *Sim's Case* in England in 1601. One scholar notes that "[t]he judges for the case expressed concern about abortions and how difficult they are to prove."[89] Indeed, we have already noted Jefferson's observations above that cases of this kind are hard to prove.[90] Not surprisingly then, most of the few abortion cases in early England resulted in acquittal due to lack of evidence--although there was one case in 1320 or 1321 in which "a person who caused an abortion was found guilty and hanged."[91]

It was this evidentiary difficulty of proof of causation that led Lord Coke in 1648 to articulate the 'born alive' rule regarding abortion: "If a woman be quick with childe, and by a potion or otherwise killeth it in her wombe, or if a man beat her, whereby the childe dyeth in her body, and she is delivered of a dead childe, this is a great misprision and no murder; but if the childe be born alive and dyeth of the potion, battery, or other cause, this is murder."[92] Hence, for Coke aborting a quick child was indeed criminal but not murder because of lack of certain proof that the fetal death was caused by the abortionist and not another cause--unless the child was born alive and then died, which was the surest proof of all for a murder conviction. Blackstone reiterated the rule from Lord Coke with very similar wording.[93]

The purely evidentiary nature of the common law abortion rule was clearly demonstrated by Blackstone on another occasion, when he described the common law rule for executing women found guilty of a capital offense, and who are pregnant. If a woman was convicted of any crime that resulted in capital punishment, the execution had to be stayed if she was pregnant until after the infant was born. Blackstone's phraseology regarding how the pregnancy was to be determined and the life of the infant protected is very insightful: "the judge must direct a jury of twelve matrons or discreet women to inquire the fact; and if they bring in their verdict quick with child,(for barely with child, *unless it be alive in the womb*, is not sufficient,) execution shall be stayed generally till the next session."[94] The term "barely with child" was obviously a reference to the first trimester and early part of the second trimester prior to quickening or movement of the fetus that could (in that day) be discerned by the outside world. Blackstone's wording indicated that if there was a way to determine that the infant was "barely with child" but was nonetheless "alive in the womb" prior to quickening, the execution would likewise be stayed and the life of the infant protected. This again brings to mind the statement of Benjamin Rush cited above, that there was constant movement by the unborn from the moment of conception, even though such movement could not be proven in that day prior to quickening, after the end of the first trimester.[95] Clearly under the common law, if movement in the womb *could* be determined earlier for evidentiary purposes, the infant was to be protected from the point at which movement could be confirmed.

An example of the application of the woman-execution law and the difficulty of such proof is seen in the story of Bethesda Spooner in Massachusetts in 1778, who claimed she was pregnant and that her sentence of hanging for murder should be stayed until after the child was born. In her pleas under the common law for a stay of execution, Bethesda urged the Executive Council charged with fulfilling her execution to protect the unborn child who had "a right to the existence which God hath begun to give it," and that the judges should "desire to preserve life, even in its miniature state, rather than to destroy it." Her minister also appealed to the court for a stay, noting that otherwise her execution would "destroy innocent life."[96] It is noteworthy that the infant was considered to be a "life" and therefore protectable in both of these statements, even though quickening of the child had not yet occurred. While two midwife examinations were undertaken, the results were mixed and the execution was therefore ordered. After Spooner's execution, it was discovered to the chagrin of all that a five month old fetus was within her.[97]

This evidentiary problem obviously does not exist today. Modern medical technology allows us to verify the common law criteria for protection--movement--from a significantly earlier period in pregnancy. With modern technology, a fetal heartbeat can be detected at about the 25th day after conception.[98] For most women, this is about the same time they even discover they are pregnant, and begin to consider whether to have an abortion. Even early abortion procedures such as the abortion pill (RU-486 or Mifeprex, not the 'morning after pill') or the aspiration procedure are almost never performed prior to this time. The fetal heartbeat is all the proof needed under the common law to show that the child is alive and merits protection. A proper interpretation of the common law accordingly *requires* protection of the unborn child from this time, and would virtually eliminate almost all abortions (other than those caused by the 'morning after pill,' in which a fertilized egg is prevented from implanting on the walls of the womb). Obviously, as medical technology improves and detection of fetal movement comes even earlier in pregnancy, this date will be moved ever closer to the date of conception.

Furthermore, modern medical technology can also usually confirm whether the effort to abort was the cause of fetal death, which was the element of proof that was lacking for criminal conviction of murder for abortion in the founding era. Accordingly, proof that an abortionist caused fetal death is not nearly as lacking as in that day, and therefore proof sufficient for a conviction for murder can now more easily be found. In short, if the *Roe* court had properly interpreted the common law rule, they once again would have been compelled to rule opposite to the way they did.

But there is more. When speaking of inheritance rights, Blackstone stated on another occasion that the common law also protected the life of unborn infants prior to quickening, and that the unborn possessed rights from the moment of conception. In another section of his Commentaries, Blackstone noted that "[a]n infant in ventre sa mere, or in the mother's womb, is supposed in law to be born for many purposes. It is capable of having a legacy ... it may have a guardian assigned to it; and it is enabled to have an estate limited to its use, and to take afterwards by such limitation, as if it were then actually born."[99] There is no quickening distinction in this statement, and the rule therefore applies from conception. Hence, an unborn child had the right at common law to inheritance and property rights from the moment of conception, as long as it was ultimately born alive.

Amazingly, the *Roe* court briefly acknowledged this point, but naturally failed to acknowledge that the protection was from the moment of conception.[100]

There is horrific inconsistency in protecting an unborn's property more assiduously than his life. Such a concept flies in the face of due process of law (the very principal relied on by the *Roe* court), which requires protection of life as well as property. Indeed, one jurist of 100 years ago noted this inconsistency by observing that under these two conflicting rules regarding the unborn "[O]ne must respect the rights of ownership, and ... disregard the safety of the owner. In such argument there is not true sense of proportion in the protection of rights. The greater is denied."[101]

Returning to James Wilson, while he articulated the common law rule with all of its evidentiary weaknesses in that day, there is no question that he agreed with his fellow founders that abortion at any stage of pregnancy is morally unacceptable. This can be seen by other comments he made. One of these was his statement against suicide, using wording that--like that of John Locke above[102]--demonstrate that only God has the right to deny a right to life once it has its start. Wilson stated:

[I]t was not by his own voluntary act that the man made his appearance upon the theater of life; he cannot, therefore, plead the right of the nation, by his own voluntary act to make his exit. He did not make; therefore, he has no right to destroy himself. *He alone, whose gift this state of existence is, has the right to say when and how it shall receive its termination.*[103]

Wilson further stated that, just as it is "the duty of a state to preserve itself; so it is, in general, its duty to preserve its members."[104] Expounding further on this point, he stated that:

This duty the nation owes to itself, because the loss of its members is a proportionate loss of its strength; and the loss of its strength is proportionably injurious both to its security, and to its preservation ... the body of a nation should not abandon ... an individual, who has not forfeited his rights in the society."[105]

This statement highlights an element of abortion that is frequently overlooked. Legally accepted abortion, such as that created in America today by the judiciary in the *Roe* decision, robs the nation of its strength. Large numbers of individuals are denied existence, who may have otherwise served the nation with strength and vigor.

Elsewhere Wilson stated that "*the moral sense restrains us from harming the innocent*; it teaches us that the innocent have a right to be secure from harm," and furthermore that we should be willing to "submit to any distress or danger, rather than procure our safety and relief by violence upon an innocent person."[106] Like Madison, he condemned the practice of infanticide in China and other countries,[107] and prefaced his statement of the common law abortion rule by noting that "life, and whatever is necessary for the safety of life, are the natural rights of man."[108] Finally, regarding illegitimate children he noted that "it is the natural duty of his parents to maintain, to protect, and to educate him."[109] All of these statements show that Wilson, like the other founding fathers, would not agree with government sanctioned abortions at any state of pregnancy.

Notes to chapter 5:

[81] McCloskey, above note 32, vol. 2, at 597 (emphasis added). An interesting variation of the rule is given in a contemporary British treatise, J. Johnson, *The Laws Respecting Women*, 348 (London, 1777). The rule states: "As soon as an infant is able to stir in its

mother's womb, it becomes an object of protection in the eye of the law ..." The evidentiary nature of the rule is highlighted since prior to 'stirring' the law could provide no protection, since its existence and status of being alive could not be confirmed.

[82] *Roe v. Wade*, 410 US 113, 133 (1973).

[83] See above note 23, and accompanying text.

[84] See above note 11, and accompanying text.

[85] Dennis J. Horan & Thomas J. Balch, "Roe v. Wade: No Basis in Law, Logic, or History," in *The Abortion Controversy: A Reader*, at 94 (Louis P. Pojman & Francis J. Beckwith, eds, 1994).

[86] Dellapenna, above note 11, at 25.

[87] James Parker, *Conductor Generalis: Or, the Office, Duty and Authority of Justices of the Peace*, at 216-217 (1764)(emphasis added).

[88] Year Book Mich., 22 Edw. 3, in Fitzherbert, *Le Graunde Abridgement*, vol. 2, fol. 217, no. 263. The case is discussed and quoted in: John M. Riddle, *Eve's Herbs: A History of Contraception and Abortion in the West*, at 96 (1997).

[89] Riddle, above note 88, at 130.

[90] See above note 51, and accompanying text.

[91] Riddle, above note 88, at 99. Riddle notes however that the person hanged was also charged with other, unspecified crimes. Riddle also referred to seven abortion cases that resulted in acquittal, apparently due to lack of evidence. Ibid.

[92] Sir Edward Coke, *Coke's Institutes*, vol. 3, at 50 (1648).

[93] 1Blackstone, *Commentaries*, vol. 1, at *129, *139 (1765).

[94] Ibid, vol. 2, at *395 (1765).

[95] See above, notes 22-23, and accompanying text.

[96] *American Criminal Trials*, vol. 2, at 1, 49-51 (Peleg Chandler ed., 1844), cited in Dellapenna, above note 11, at 225-26.

[97] Dellapenna, above note 11, at 226.

[98] "One of the important aspects of diagnosing a live intrauterine pregnancy is the timing of appearance of the fetal heartbeat ... this appears around day 25 postconception ... we consider the appearance of the heartbeat to be the first positive sign of a live pregnancy." Natan Haratz-Rubinstein & Ilan E. Timor-

Tritsch, "The Role of Ultrasound in Oocyte Donation Programs," in *Principles of Oocyte and Embryo Donation*, at 144 (Mark V. Sauer, ed., 1998).

[99] 1 Blackstone, *Commentaries*, at *126 (1765)). The only requirement Blackstone identified was that the child later be born alive. Ibid.

[100] *Roe v. Wade*, 410 US 113, 162 (1973).

[101] *Nugent v. Brooklyn Heights Railroad Co.*, 154 App. Div. 667, 672; 139 NYS 367, 371 (1913). The case was for negligent harm to an unborn by a railroad. The court ruled that under the rules of negligence, the Railroad did not have a duty to scrutinize passengers, looking for unborns to whom it would owe a duty if they were injured.

[102] See above, note 70, and accompanying text.

[103] McCloskey, above note 32, vol. 1, at 155 (emphasis added).

[104] Ibid., at 156.

[105] Ibid.

[106] Ibid., at 232-33 (emphasis added).

[107] Ibid., at 245; McCloskey, above note 32, vol. 2, at 597.

[108] McCloskey, above note 32, vol. 2, at 596.

[109] Ibid., at 605.

CHAPTER 6: A PROPER UNDERSTANDING OF NATURAL LAW AND THE COMMON LAW

Especially when it comes to abortion, it is essential to understand the distinction between natural law and the common law. As indicated above, the common law is only used when no other law exists regarding a subject. Courts will only invoke the common law if the legislature has not made a law about the issue, and if there is no constitutional provision about it either. As such, the common law is at the lowest level of law. It is at the bottom of the legal food chain, and is subject to change at any time by the legislature or the courts.[110]

Natural law on the other hand, is at the highest level, and cannot be changed except by God. The founders considered natural law to be superior to legislation and even to the constitution itself. It was natural law that justified America's revolt from England, in direct defiance of the British constitution, British statutes, and the British common law. Thomas Jefferson articulated this concept in the Declaration of Independence, stating that it was natural law that entitled the people to form a new government.[111] Accordingly, if a court must decide an issue that is found only in natural law and in the common law, it should follow natural law in its ruling rather than the common law. The Supreme Court in *Roe* did the opposite.

The natural law rights referred to in the Ninth Amendment are not stray principles that men can make up at a whim, or derive from popular sentiment of the day. The Ninth Amendment was to be anchored to the natural law understanding of the founding generation. The Ninth Amendment states that "the enumeration in the Constitution of certain rights shall not be construed to deny or disparage others retained by the people." Lawyers know that language such as this which refers to outside principles or facts is simply an "incorporation by reference" clause. In this case, it is intended to incorporate other identifiable rights as they existed *as of that date*, and not rights that could be invented by future generations. No lawyer in his right mind would insert an "incorporation by reference" clause that was intended to incorporate future understandings, since that would undermine the entire contract, rendering it unenforceable. To be a valid and enforceable "incorporation by reference" clause, the provisions to be incorporated must exist at the time the clause is adopted, and must thereafter be followed. In the case of the Ninth Amendment, this is the natural law understanding of the founding generation. The founders would never have been so foolish as to insert a provision in the constitution that was so open-ended it could undermine the entire structure. They never had any intention that natural law incorporated by the Ninth Amendment would change according to the whims of men. For them, natural law was the law of God, which does not and cannot change.

The understanding of natural law rights of the founders which we are to follow can be found in their writings and in the writings of Locke and the other natural law writers, as described above. Indeed, natural law rights were seen by the founders as being "engraven by God on the hearts of all men."[112] As Alexander Hamilton put it, natural law rights "are written, as with a sunbeam, in the whole volume of human nature, by the hand of the divinity itself."[113]

It must be emphasized again that the founders intended for succeeding generations of Americans to continually honor and respect the natural law rights understanding of the founding generation, rather than try to make up new rights on their own. Indeed, given the founders' understanding of the divine and unchangeable nature of natural law rights as articulated above, they did not see how such rights could ever be changed from the ones they understood in their day. These were principles of morality that were fixed, eternal, and never changing. Regarding such moral principles, George Washington said "A good general government, without good morals and good habits, will not make us a happy people; and we shall deceive ourselves if we think it will."[114]

The founders clearly articulated the principal that succeeding generations were to be anchored to the founders' understanding of natural law and the constitution. James Madison, father of the constitution, stated regarding the original intent of the founders that "The [governmental] improvements made by the dead form a debt against the living, who take the benefit of them. This debt cannot be otherwise discharged than by a proportionate *obedience to the will of the Authors* of the improvements."[115] Madison made it clear that the 'improvements' he was talking about were the governmental structure and rights set in place by the founding generation, including the natural law rights incorporated by the Ninth Amendment. Jefferson concurred, noting that "On every question of construction, [let us] carry ourselves back to the time when the Constitution was adopted, recollect the spirit manifested in the debates, and instead of trying what meaning may be squeezed out of the text, or invented against it, conform to the probable one in which it was passed."[116] This statement is equally true of the Ninth

Amendment, and the unlisted natural rights incorporated by reference that it was intended to protect. There is no need to resort to the due process clause of the Fourteenth Amendment or the common law to protect such rights--by the founders' design, all such unlisted and unenumerated rights are protected by the Ninth Amendment.[117]

Once again, natural law rights were seen by the founders as the highest level of law, and were clearly against abortion from the moment of conception. Contrast this with the British common law. It is well known that the common law is only good until it is overturned by legislative enactment or court decree. In direct contrast to natural law which is the highest form of law and is unalterable, the common law is the lowest and most inferior form of law, being below natural law, constitutional law, and legislation. The view of the common law as being inferior to all other competing forms of law persists to this day.[118] Obviously, if there is ever a conflict between a natural law and the common law, natural law must prevail.

James Madison described the common law as being full of "incongruities, barbarisms, and bloody maxims," concluding that "the common law never was, nor by any fair construction ever can be, deemed a law for the American people."[119]   Madison was particularly firm that the Supreme Court should not interpret the common law as support for a constitutional right--*which is exactly what occurred in Roe v. Wade.* Indeed, in words that sound precisely like a modern day criticism of *Roe,* he stated:

Whether the common law be admitted as of legal or of constitutional obligation, it would confer on the judicial department a discretion little short of a legislative power ... [they would] decide what parts of the common law would, and what would not, be properly applicable to the circumstances of the United States. A discretion of this sort has always been lamented as incongruous and dangerous ... the power of the judges over the law would, in fact, erect them into legislators, and ... it would be impossible for the citizens to conjecture, either what was or would be law.[120]

Notwithstanding Madison's warnings, this is exactly what happened in the *Roe* decision. Five unelected judges legislated for the entire country, defying and destroying dozens of state laws on abortion. They did so on the basis that there was somehow a constitutional right to an abortion derived from the common law. And in so doing, they completely ignored the natural law rights of the unborn to protection under the Ninth Amendment.

Notes to chapter 6:

[110] *American Jurisprudence Second,* "Common Law", vol. 15, at §15 (2000).

[111] In speaking in the opening paragraph of the people having the right to "dissolve the political bands" which connected them to Britain, Jefferson noted that the people have the right "to assume among the powers of the earth, the separate and equal station to which

the Laws of Nature and of Nature's God entitle them." Declaration of Independence, ¶ 1.

[112] McCloskey, above note 32, vol. 1, at 102.

[113] Hamilton, above note 30, vol. 2, at 80.

[114] Letter of Aug. 31, 1788, from George Washington to Annis Boudinot Stockton, found in Fitzpatrick, above note 31, vol. 30, at 76.

[115] Letter from James Madison to Thomas Jefferson, Feb. 4, 1790, found in Hunt, above note 29, vol. 5, at 439 (emphasis added).

[116] Letter from Thomas Jefferson to William Johnson, June 12, 1823, found in Ford, above note 14, vol. 10, at 231.

[117] While the *Roe* majority based their decision on the Fourteenth Amendment, they did briefly mention the Ninth Amendment. *Roe v. Wade*, 410 US 113, 129 (1973). However,

they did not make the Ninth Amendment the basis of their decision and their statements about the Ninth Amendment indicate that they misinterpreted it.

[118] *American Jurisprudence Second,* "Common Law", vol. 15, at §15 (2000).

[119] Hunt, above note 29, vol. 6, at 380-81.

[120] Ibid., at 378, 380-81.

CHAPTER 7: CONCLUSION

From all of the above, it can be seen that the founding fathers disagreed with abortion at every stage after conception. They viewed abortion as just another unacceptable form of infanticide. Any alleged "right" to an abortion would have to be derived from natural law as incorporated by the Ninth Amendment--and no such right existed. On the contrary, natural law protects the right of the unborn, not the whims of the mother to terminate that life. Abortion is a flagrant violation of the natural law the founders firmly believed in, as expressed by John Locke and other natural law writers.

The simple reality is that the founders intended for the Ninth Amendment to incorporate natural law as they understood it in their day, and therefore the Ninth Amendment protects the natural right to life of each unborn infant from the moment of conception. Anything less than this is a defiance of the constitution and the intent of the founders. In short, the *Roe* court blasphemed the constitution, and ruled directly opposite to the way it should have.

In reviewing the unlisted rights under the Ninth Amendment of the Constitution to see if the right to abortion was among them, the founders would never have resorted to elevation of the common law over natural law as the

Supreme Court did in *Roe v. Wade*. They would have done the opposite and would have turned to natural law to see if it supported or opposed abortion. As has abundantly been seen above, natural law was squarely against abortion, and in fact protects the rights of the unborn from conception onward. Hence, the founding fathers would have viewed the *Roe* court's reliance on the common law and its ruling as turning the question on its head, and denying protection to the innocent unborns who were to be constitutionally preserved.

But this not all. Even if the Ninth Amendment and the intent of the framers can somehow be ignored, a proper understanding of the common law itself shows that it is strongly against abortion. The common law abortion rule was based on evidentiary standards of that day, and was all about finding proof sufficient to obtain criminal conviction for a serious crime. If properly applied in modern times with the aid of modern medical science, the common law is strongly against abortion. Hence, the *Roe* decision was not only an egregious departure from the views of the founding fathers and a gross violation of the constitution, but was a defiance of the very common law the *Roe* court relied on.

There is no question that if the founding fathers were alive today, they would lament the senseless loss of constitutional protections for the unborn, and the needless slaughter of millions of innocent lives. They would vigorously oppose abortion 'law' in America today.

ABOUT THE AUTHOR: Duane L. Ostler practiced law in the USA for 11 years before obtaining a PhD in legal history. Feel free to contact Mr. Ostler at: duanelostler@gmail.com.

OTHER BOOKS BY THE AUTHOR:

Nonfiction:

James Madison, American Prophet

Rather amazingly, James Madison foresaw many of the problems we face in America today. He foresaw our modern obsession with individual rights, the dangers of judicial activism, the problems of a war presidency, and the economic difficulties that can bring a nation to ruin. Most importantly, as America's preeminent political visionary, he also saw how these problems can be solved.

The Ninth Amendment: Key to Understanding the Bill of Rights

This book explains how the Ninth Amendment is the key to understanding rights in the United States. The founders created the Ninth Amendment to protect unlisted natural law rights as they were understood in their day. This amendment was never intended to allow future generations to create new rights. Rather, it was to safeguard the morality and natural rights of the founding generation.

A Conversation About Abortion Between Justice Blackmun and the Founding Fathers

On a dark night in Independence Hall, ghosts of the founding fathers gather to discuss with Justice Blackmun the Roe v Wade abortion opinion he penned in 1973. Using actual quotes from the founding fathers, this debate soundly refutes Blackmun's arguments from the Roe opinion, and shows that the founders would be greatly disturbed at the law regarding abortion in America today.

The Government Took My Property! A Comparison of Acquisition Law in Australia and the United States (under pen name "Silas Flint")

Most people don't think much about acquisitions or "takings" of private property by the government--until they receive a letter that their land is about to be taken! This complex subject is made easy to understand in this volume. The author uses zany humor and bizarre examples to describe the history of acquisitions in Australia and the USA, and how they have come to be what they are today.

Fiction:

<u>My Science Teacher is a Wizard</u>
<u>My Math Teacher is a Vampire</u>
<u>My History Teacher is a Leprechaun</u>
<u>My English Teacher is a Werewolf</u>
<u>The Wards of Clovis Gloober</u>
<u>Detectives in Diapers: They Mystery of the Aztec Amulet</u>
<u>Itchy Mitch and the Taming of Broken Jaw Junction</u>
<u>Santa v Afton (under pen name "Silas Flint")</u>
<u>Running for the Guv (under pen name "Silas Flint")</u>